AMAZING ANIMALS

SUGAR GLIDERS

BY MARI BOLTE

CREATIVE EDUCATION • CREATIVE PAPERBACKS

Published by Creative Education
and Creative Paperbacks
P.O. Box 227, Mankato, Minnesota 56002
Creative Education and Creative Paperbacks
are imprints of The Creative Company
www.thecreativecompany.us

Design by The Design Lab
Production by Blue Design
Art direction by Wyeth Morgan

Getty Images/Kristina Parchomchuk, 7, kuritafsheen, 9, McDonald Wildlife Photography Inc., 16, Moonstone Images, 18, somnuk krobkum, 13, Wong Yu Liang, 23; Shutterstock/Nynke van Holten, cover, 1; Unsplash/David Clode, 14, Timur Garifov, 2, 20; Wikimedia Commons/Garst, Warren, 5, Greg Tasney, 21, Matteo De Stefano/MUSE, 2, 3, 4, 6, 7, 8, 10, 11, 12, 13, 14, 15, 16, 18, 19, 20, 21, 22, 24, Mew Pet Shop, 10, patrickkavanagh, 6, Wm Jas /Tai Bingyou, 17

Library of Congress Cataloging-in-Publication Data
Names: Bolte, Mari author
Title: Sugar gliders / by Mari Bolte.
Description: Mankato, Minnesota : Creative Education and Creative Paperbacks, [2026] | Series: Amazing animals | Includes bibliographical references and index. | Audience: Ages 6-9 | Audience: Grades 2-3 | Summary: "Discover the fascinating world of sugar gliders with this engaging title for elementary-aged readers. Learn about sugar gliders' habitats, behaviors, and unique traits, and enjoy a captivating tale about their symbolic significance in Australian culture"– Provided by publisher.
Identifiers: LCCN 2025011196 (print) | LCCN 2025011197 (ebook) | ISBN 9798895810606 library binding | ISBN 9798896800132 paperback | ISBN 9798895811863 ebook
Subjects: LCSH: Sugar glider–Juvenile literature
Classification: LCC QL737.M373 B65 2026 (print) | LCC QL737.M373 (ebook) | DDC 599.2/3–dc23/eng/20250618
LC record available at https://lccn.loc.gov/2025011196
LC ebook record available at https://lccn.loc.gov/2025011197

Printed in China

Table of Contents

Sugar gliders can float as far as 165 feet (50.3 meters).

Sugar gliders are tiny **marsupials**. They live in Australia and New Guinea. They have excellent eyesight, especially at night when they are most active. During the day, they sleep in leafy nests built in hollow trees.

marsupial a mammal that carries its young in a pouch

Sugar gliders weigh 3 to 5 ounces (85 to 142 grams).

Sugar gliders get their name from their ability to glide through the air. They have special **membranes** between their wrists and ankles that look like wings. They also have flat, bushy tails. Both membranes and tails help them steer while they float.

membrane a thin, flexible layer of skin

Flying squirrels, flying lemurs, and sugar gliders are the only mammals that glide. Even though they are similar, they are not related. Sugar gliders are closer cousins to koalas and kangaroos.

Sugar gliders have five toes on each foot. They can grab, which helps sugar gliders land smoothly.

A sugar glider's tail is one and a half times longer than its body.

Sugar gliders come in many different colors. Gray is the most common. It helps them hide from **predators**. They have darker stripes that run from head to tail. Their tails can carry light things, such as twigs or leaves.

predator an animal that eats other animals

Sugar gliders live in tropical eucalyptus and acacia forests. They are omnivores. Nectar, pollen, and gum from trees are their main meals. Fruit and tree nuts are other options. They also eat insects, spiders, and even small birds.

nectar a sugary fluid that comes from plants

omnivore an animal that eats both plants and animals

As long as there are trees, sugar gliders can make a nest. They have even been found in cities.

Sugar gliders live in families of up to seven adults and their babies. They share a single nest and protect their territories from other clans. Males mark trees with urine and saliva. They also have scent glands in their heads, feet, and bottoms.

saliva watery liquid that comes from glands in the mouth

scent glands skin glands that produce liquids with unique smells

Sugar gliders mate once or twice a year. Females are pregnant for 15 to 17 days. Their tiny babies are called joeys. After they are born, they crawl to their mother's pouch. They stay there for two months. Females can carry babies from different litters at the same time.

Sugar gliders have one to two babies at a time.

Predators like snakes, owls, foxes, and cats like to snack on sugar gliders. On the ground, sugar gliders are not fast. But they can run away and glide to a different tree when threatened. Traveling through the air also keeps them out of reach of ground predators.

Young sugar gliders are easy prey for hungry hunters.

Sugar gliders are noisy! They bark, purr, chirp, and hiss. Some noises are warnings a predator is nearby. Others are calls for help or to scare other sugar gliders away. Female sugar gliders sing to their joeys to comfort them.

A high-pitched noise called crabbing tells others that they are unhappy.

A Sugar Glider Tale

Every summer, from November to April, monsoons hit Australia's Daly River region. These heavy rains bring fresh water to the land. But they are also dangerous. One legend says it is a sugar glider that travels across the sky, moving clouds across the land.